Western tiger swallowtail butterfly

Twenty thousand species of butterflies brighten the world. As you can see, butterflies have a wonderful variety of colors, wing shapes, and sizes. The largest is the *Queen Alexandra birdwing*. It has a bigger wingspan than many birds. The world's smallest butterfly, the *small blue*, measures less than an inch from wingtip to wingtip.

No two butterflies of the same species are exactly alike. Each is a bit different from the other. Often, the most colorful butterflies are males. Females tend to be duller looking, which lets them blend in with their surroundings. This helps to protect them from predators while laying their eggs. But whether male or female, large or small, the fluttering and soaring butterflies make fields, forests, and mountainsides come alive!

CRACKER BUTTERFLY
Hamadryas chloe
(South and Central America)

NORTH AMERICAN TIGER SWALLOWTAIL
Papilio glaucus
(North America)

GOLD-SPOT SKIPPER
Aguna asander
(North America)

CABBAGE BUTTERFLY
Artogeia rapae
(North America)

PEACOCK BUTTERFLY
Inachis io
(Europe)

TREE NYMPH
Idea leuconoe
(Southeast Asia)

QUEEN ALEXANDRA BIRDWING (MALE)
Ornithoptera alexandrae
(New Guinea)

COMMON BLUEBOTTLE
Graphium sarpedon
(Australia to India)

DOG FACE BUTTERFLY
Zerene cesonia
(Southwestern United States)

**AUSTRALIAN
REGENT SKIPPER**
Euschemon rafflesia
(Australia)

PAINTED LADY
Vanessa cardui
(North and South
America, Europe,
Africa, Asia, and
Australia)

GREAT NORTHERN SULPHER
Colias gigantea
(Arctic North America)

**BLOOD-RED
CYMOTHOE**
Cymothoe sangaris
(Africa)

CITRUS SWALLOWTAIL
Papilio demodocus
(Africa)

**QUEEN ALEXANDRA
BIRDWING (FEMALE)**
Ornithoptera alexandrae
(New Guinea)

The largest butterfly in the world
is the female *Queen Alexandra
birdwing*, with a wingspan of
11 inches. The world's smallest
butterfly is probably the *small blue*.
It is so tiny that it could fit on the
tip of your nose!

SMALL BLUE
Philotiella speciosa
(Asia and Europe)

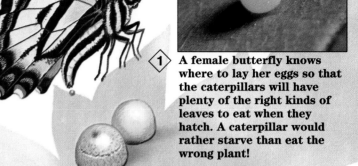

*L*ike magic, a butterfly changes from a sluggish caterpillar into a beautiful, graceful adult. This magic of nature is called *metamorphosis*. The reason it seems like magic is because the immature or larval stage in this development—the caterpillar—is completely unlike the adult butterfly. Looks, life-styles, and eating habits are different.

There are four stages in a butterfly's life cycle. The first is the *egg* laid by the female. After 5 to 10 days, a tiny *caterpillar* hatches from the egg. The caterpillar begins an eating binge that continues through its stage in a butterfly's life. The well-fed caterpillar now sustains life through the next stage of development—the *pupa* or *chrysalis*. During this dormant but transitional stage, no food is taken in. At the end of this stage, transformation is complete, and the *adult butterfly* emerges from the chrysalis. If conditions are unfavorable at any stage, development may be delayed until conditions improve.

1 A female butterfly knows where to lay her eggs so that the caterpillars will have plenty of the right kinds of leaves to eat when they hatch. A caterpillar would rather starve than eat the wrong plant!

Butterfly eggs, like the ones above, come in many shapes and textures. Some are smooth, while others have grooves on the surface.

2 After several days, the egg is ready to hatch. Then the caterpillar eats its way out of the egg, head first.

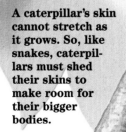

Caterpillars are eating machines. They have massive jaws for munching leaves. In their short lifetime, they may eat as much as *20 times their weight* in food.

3 Once free of the egg, the caterpillar turns and eats its shell. The egg-shell provides important nutrients that the caterpillar will need to keep growing.

Before shedding its skin for the last time, the caterpillar attaches itself to a stem by spinning a silk "button." Once secure, it wiggles out of its old skin to expose a tough new skin. This new skin hardens almost immediately– it is called a *chrysalis.*

5

4 A caterpillar's skin cannot stretch as it grows. So, like snakes, caterpillars must shed their skins to make room for their bigger bodies.

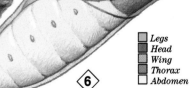

☐ Legs
☐ Head
☐ Wing
☐ Thorax
☐ Abdomen

6 Inside the chrysalis, the caterpillar's eyes, legs, and body are broken down into a thick liquid. Slowly, the parts of the adult butterfly begin to form. This process may take days, weeks, or even months. Can you make out the parts of the developing butterfly in the chrysalis above?

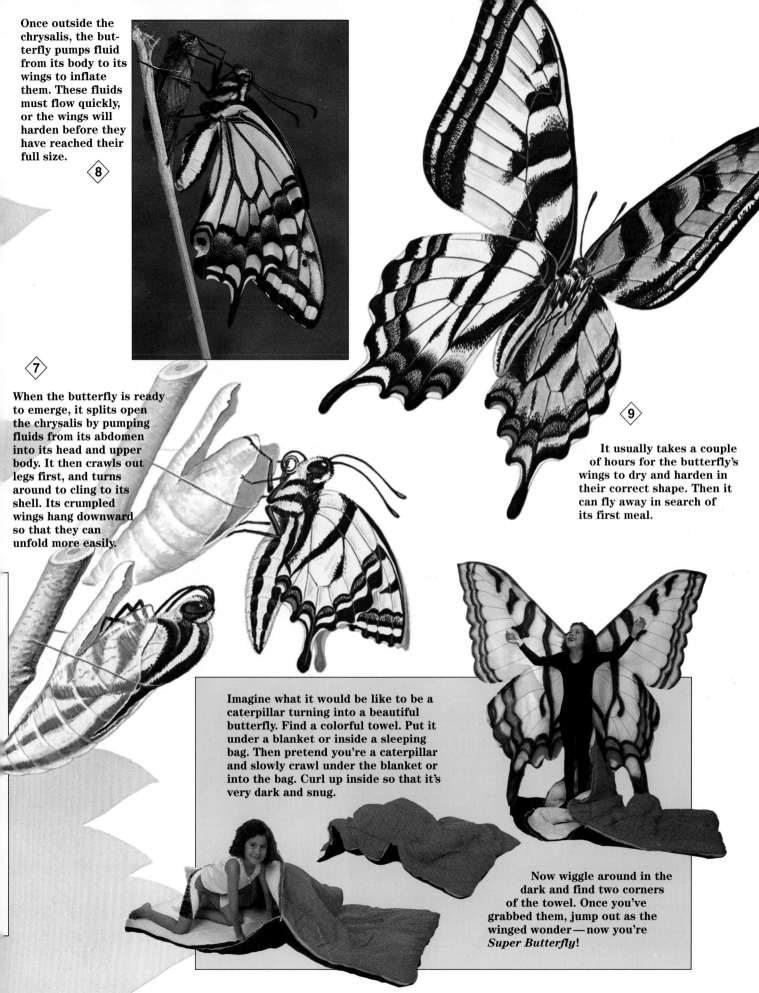

Once outside the chrysalis, the butterfly pumps fluid from its body to its wings to inflate them. These fluids must flow quickly, or the wings will harden before they have reached their full size.

⟨8⟩

⟨7⟩

When the butterfly is ready to emerge, it splits open the chrysalis by pumping fluids from its abdomen into its head and upper body. It then crawls out legs first, and turns around to cling to its shell. Its crumpled wings hang downward so that they can unfold more easily.

⟨9⟩

It usually takes a couple of hours for the butterfly's wings to dry and harden in their correct shape. Then it can fly away in search of its first meal.

Imagine what it would be like to be a caterpillar turning into a beautiful butterfly. Find a colorful towel. Put it under a blanket or inside a sleeping bag. Then pretend you're a caterpillar and slowly crawl under the blanket or into the bag. Curl up inside so that it's very dark and snug.

Now wiggle around in the dark and find two corners of the towel. Once you've grabbed them, jump out as the winged wonder—now you're *Super Butterfly*!

A butterfly's structure may seem unusual, but it makes perfect sense for the butterfly. Butterflies taste with their feet, smell with their antennae, and carry their own straws for sipping nectar!

The most noticeable thing about a butterfly is its striking color. The tiny scales that cover a butterfly's wings give it color and iridescence. Colors serve many purposes in a butterfly's life. They can attract a mate, warn off a predator, and help the butterfly blend in with its surroundings.

A butterfly's body has three sections. Its *head* carries the coiled drinking tube and several sensory devices for selecting food sources, providing balance, a sense of smell, and orientation during flight. Its *thorax* anchors the butterfly's four wings and the six legs that walk and cling. (The feet carry sense organs for taste.) Its *abdomen* holds scent glands and reproductive organs.

Here is a closeup view of a butterfly's scales. You can see how they overlap like shingles on a roof. Underneath the scales, butterfly wings are clear and thin like cellophane.

Moth antennae come in all shapes and sizes. Some are ordinary, but many are feathered and fringed. Because moths are active at night, they need extra sensitive antennae for locating food and mates. Butterflies have simpler, knobbed antennae. But butterflies are active in the daytime and can also rely on sight.

The moth is the butterfly's closest relative. Here are a few simple ways to tell moths and butterflies apart.

Most moths have fatter bodies than butterflies do. And they are usually much less colorful.

As incredible as it sounds, a butterfly *tastes with its feet*! As soon as it lands on a flower, it uses its feet, called *tarsi*, to tell whether this is the flower it wants. If you tasted your food the way a butterfly does, you would have to put your toes in your dessert to sample it!

A butterfly's skeleton is on the *outside* of its body, instead of on the inside like yours. It is called an *exoskeleton*. It provides the insect with a hard, protective covering for its soft insides.

Have you ever seen a butterfly resting on the ground with its wings wide open? It's soaking up the sun's heat. Butterflies are cold-blooded animals and need to warm themselves in the sunshine before they can fly away.

Although butterflies cannot fly as fast as birds, they use their wings in the same way to flutter, glide, and soar. And the fastest insects, including some of the tropical butterflies, can maintain a flying speed of 24 miles per hour!

Butterflies smell with their antennae to find nectar. Females locate plants where they deposit their eggs. And males use their antennae to detect the scent of females for mating. A special organ at the base of the antennae helps butterflies to orient themselves during flight.

To sip nectar, butterflies have a long hollow tube called a *proboscis*. This lets them probe deep into flowers to reach the nectar. When the proboscis is not being used, it stays coiled up underneath the butterfly's head.

SEE FOR YOURSELF

Would you like to try drinking like a butterfly? First, connect three or four drinking straws so that they become one long straw.

Fill a glass with fruit juice. Put one end of your giant straw into the glass and suck from the other end. Can you imagine drinking all your meals like this?

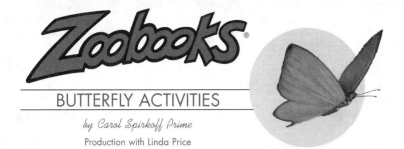

Zoobooks®

BUTTERFLY ACTIVITIES

by Carol Spirkoff Prime
Production with Linda Price

☆ **BONUS ACTIVITIES** ☆

Don't flutter by these fun activities without trying them. We've added these four extra pages to enhance your experiences with *Zoobooks®*. We hope you enjoy these projects.

Carol Spirkoff Prime is a nationally recognized educational writer. As a lecturer and supervisor in the College of Education at San Diego State University, she helps prepare future teachers.

A Royal Traveler

Every year this butterfly with a royal name makes an incredible journey. Although it is still a mystery how this type of butterfly navigates, you can make your way through this puzzle by following the directions on the right. The result will be a picture of this royal traveler. See if you can find the name of this royal traveler in the pages of this book. *(Answer is on page d.)*

You will need yellow, orange, black, and brown felt pens to complete this puzzle. Then, color the squares in the grid as directed. For example, in Row 1, you will use black to color the squares in columns A and B. In Row 2, you will color the squares in columns A, C, D, T, U, and V black and the square in column B yellow. When you're finished, be sure to add antennae.

Color these squares:

Row 1 **Black:** A B

Row 2 **Black:** A C D T U V **Yellow:** B

Row 3 **Black:** A B D E R S T V W **Yellow:** C
Orange: U

Row 4 **Black:** B C F R T U W **Yellow:** S
Orange: D E V

Row 5 **Black:** B D E G Q S T V **Yellow:** F R U
White: C

Row 6 **Black:** C F G P R U V **Orange:** D E Q S T

Row 7 **Black:** C G H P U V **Orange:** D E F Q R S T

Row 8 **Black:** D H O U **Orange:** E F G P Q R S T

Row 9 **Black:** E I O U **Orange:** F G H P Q R S T

Row 10 **Black:** E J N U **Orange:** F G H I O P Q R S T

Row 11 **Black:** E F K N T **Orange:** G H I J O P Q R S

Row 12 **Black:** F G H N S **Orange:** I J K O P Q R
Brown: L M

Row 13 **Black:** G H I J K N O P Q R S T **Brown:** L M

Row 14 **Black:** G U **Orange:** H I J K N O P Q R S T
Brown: L M

Row 15 **Black:** F V **Orange:** G H I J K N O P Q R S T U
Brown: L M

Row 16 **Black:** E V **Orange:** F G H I J K N O P Q R S
T U **Brown:** L M

Row 17 **Black:** E V **Orange:** F G H I J K N O P Q R S
T U **Brown:** L M

Row 18 **Black:** E K N V **Orange:** F G H I J O P Q R S
T U **Brown:** L M

Row 19 **Black:** F J O U **Orange:** G H I P Q R S T
Brown: L M

Row 20 **Black:** G J P U **Orange:** H I Q R S T
Brown: L M

Row 21 **Black:** G H I Q R S T

Next Step: Did you know that you were practicing a map-reading skill while you were solving this puzzle? Maps are made on a grid like the one shown above. Numbers and letters usually go down the side and across the top of the maps. Then, places shown on the maps are assigned numbers and letters according to the square in which they are located.

If you look in the index of an atlas, you will find a list of place names. Each place will be followed by a number and letter, as well as the number for the map on which they can be found. For example, an index might list *Los Angeles, C5 366*. You would look at the map on page 366 and find the square for *C5*. Inside this square, you would find Los Angeles.

See if you could be a royal traveler by finding the following places in an atlas. Many of these cities have been in the news lately: Washington, D.C.; Moscow; Tokyo; Grozny; Algiers; London; Mexico City; and Sarajevo.

a

SAVE THE EARTH: ORGANIC GARDENING

Anne prized her garden. She especially enjoyed the butterflies that would flutter from flower to flower. Then one day, she noticed that something was eating her treasured plants. "Mom! What am I going to do? Something is ruining my garden!"

Anne's mother offered to spray the garden to kill the insects that were eating the plants. Anne agreed that this would be a good idea.

The day after her mother sprayed the garden with a pesticide, a kind of poison, Anne found several dead butterflies. Alarmed, she cried, "Now something is killing the butterflies in my garden!" What do you think killed the butterflies?

To Anne's surprise, the pesticide used to kill the insects that were eating the plants also killed the butterflies she cherished. After talking about the effects of the poison that they used, Anne and her family came up with a list of alternative choices that they will try in the future. These choices will not harm the environment or the animals that live in it.

Look over Anne's list. Put a check in front of the ones that you and your family could try in your own garden. Add a few ideas of your own.

- ☐ Protect plants by spraying them with soapy water.
- ☐ Put plants that naturally protect each other together in your garden.
- ☐ Introduce beneficial insects into your garden. For example, lady bugs eat other insects that would eat your plants.
- ☐ Keep your yard clean, which will reduce the number of pests.
- ☐ Regularly spray your plants with water to wash off insects.
- ☐ Use compost instead of fertilizer.
- ☐ Make an organic insect spray (see *Next Step*).
- ☐ Read a book about organic gardening.

Next Step: Here is a recipe for an insect spray that will not harm the environment but will keep many pests away from your plants. *You will need: 5 cloves garlic, 1/4 cup crushed red chilies, and 1 quart warm water. Crush the garlic, and then add it and the red chilies to the warm water. Let the mixture brew, like tea, for 24 hours. Spray plants with the solution. You will have to use this insect spray more often than you would a pesticide.*

Ask Joan Embery

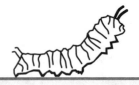

Dear Readers,

Thank you for all the cards and letters that you sent me asking questions about butterflies. Because of space, I can only answer a few of your questions each month. Nonetheless, I look forward to hearing from you.

Why do butterflies leave behind a kind of film when you touch them?
Jacey K. from Wayne, Nebraska

The wings, bodies, and legs of butterflies are covered with tiny scales that come off when they are handled. In fact, the name Lepidoptera, which is the insect order to which butterflies belong, comes from the Greek words meaning "scaly wing." When touching a butterfly, you must be very careful not to damage its delicate wings and antennae.

My mom says that there were more butterflies around when she was younger. What can we do to protect butterflies? *Matthew P. from Durango, Colorado*

We live in a complex ecosystem. Anything we do to one part of that system can affect all the other parts. As you know, the actions of people can harm the animals that live around us. Your mother has noticed one of the effects of harmful decisions made by people. But people can also make helpful decisions. For example, the people who live in the town of Pacific Grove, California, value the monarch butterflies so much that they decided to pass a law protecting these yearly visitors. There is a $500 fine or a six-month jail sentence for killing a monarch. Communities across America can decide to pass laws protecting the monarch and other butterflies. Individuals can take care not to harm these precious animals.

Please send your questions about old world monkeys to:
Ask Joan Embery
Zoobooks®
9820 Willow Creek Road
Suite 300
San Diego, CA 92131

Sincerely,

Joan Embery

Build a Butterfly Farm

You can build a butterfly farm and watch caterpillars change into butterflies. You will need: *a large box, a hammer, a nail, a jar with a lid, scissors, tape, a sheet of clear plastic (try to recycle a clear plastic bag).*

1. Ask an adult to help you poke several holes in the box so that the caterpillars can breathe. Then, have the adult make four large holes in the lid of the jar with the nail. Fill the jar with water and replace the lid.

2. Collect some caterpillars and the parts of the plants that they are on. Stick the stems of the plants through the holes in the jar lid. The stems should be long enough so that the plants will stay in the water. Place the jar inside the box.

3. Cut the sheet of clear plastic so that it is large enough to cover the side of the box. Tape it over the ends of the box so that the caterpillars can't get out, but you can see in.

4. Watch the caterpillars grow each day. Make sure they always have enough food. Be sure to keep the box out of direct sunlight so the caterpillars don't get too hot.

In time, some of the caterpillars will change into a chrysalis. This may take anywhere from a few days to several weeks. As soon as the butterflies emerge, remove the clear plastic. Watch, **but do not touch,** as the butterflies dry and fly away.

Color the Butterflies

Parents, *try these activities with your young children:*

 You can help your child make a colorful butterfly to hang in a window of your home. You will need: *colored tissue paper, scissors, black construction paper, a paintbrush, liquid starch or very thin white glue (mix equal amounts of white glue and water), waxed paper.*

Follow these steps:

1. Cut the tissue paper into 30 2-inch squares. Use many different colors.
2. Fold a piece of black construction paper in half. Then, fold it in half again. Next, trace the shape shown in Figure A onto the paper. Make sure the shape begins and ends on a fold. Help your child cut on the line you have drawn.

Figure A   Figure B

3. Help your child make several cuts of different shapes and sizes in the folded piece of black paper. See Figure B for

ideas, although very young children will probably cut fewer and larger shapes than shown. Then, open the cut paper and have your child describe the lacy butterfly.

4. Place the butterfly on a piece of waxed paper. Have your child use a paintbrush to spread starch or thin white glue over one side of the butterfly. Next, have him or her put squares of tissue all over it. Make sure that all the cutout areas are covered by tissue. Then, have your child put a final coat of starch or glue over the whole butterfly.
5. When the design is dry, lift it off the waxed paper. Invite your child to tape the butterfly to a window for your whole family to enjoy.

 Encourage your child to make up a story based on the pictures on pages 2 and 3 of this issue. Either write down the story as your child tells it or allow him or her to tape it (audio and video recordings both work well).

Caterpillar Cafe

You can open a caterpillar and butterfly restaurant. You will need: *a garden pot, potting soil, seeds.*

Choose seeds from the menus below. All of these seeds will grow into plants that are favorite foods of caterpillars and butterflies. Caterpillars will munch on the leaves, while butterflies will flock to the flowers.

Place the potting soil in the garden pot. Add water to soak the soil. Plant the seeds according to the directions on the seed packages.

Be sure to water the plants when they sprout, but not too much. Water them again each time the soil feels dry. Soon your garden will be full of color and activity.

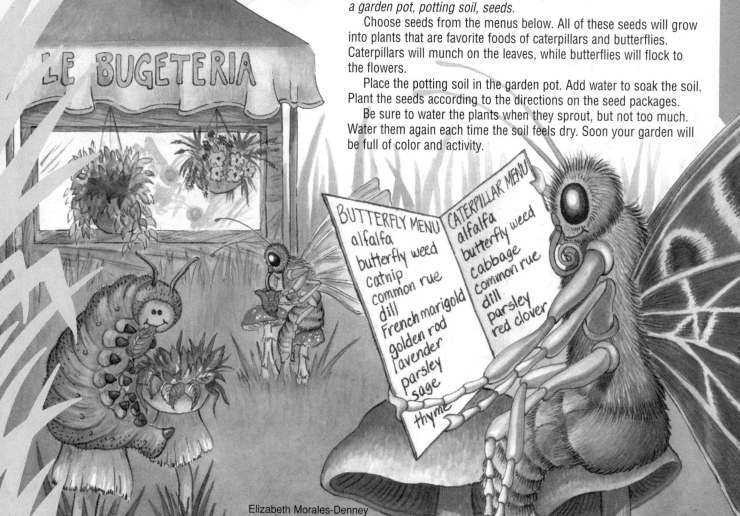

BUTTERFLY MENU
alfalfa
butterfly weed
catnip
common rue
dill
French marigold
golden rod
lavender
parsley
sage
thyme

CATERPILLAR MENU
alfalfa
butterfly weed
cabbage
common rue
dill
parsley
red clover

Elizabeth Morales-Denney

c

Mirror, Mirror on the Wall

Have you ever noticed how the wings of a butterfly appear to be reflections of each other? You can demonstrate this yourself by holding a small mirror along the dotted line on the half of a butterfly immediately below. See how the two sides look identical. Draw the missing half of the butterfly to show its mirror image.

Continue experimenting with mirror images by completing all of the activities on this page. You will need a small mirror with a flat edge and a pencil or felt pen. Place the mirror along the dotted line in each example to see the image and its reflection. Each image will help you learn more about butterflies and reflections.

Answers are on page b.

What animal is the butterfly's closest relative? (Finish the letters to write the answer.) →

M O T H

What's the best way to hunt a butterfly? ↓ (Find the mirror image of each incomplete letter to write the answer.)

W I T H A C A M E R A

Which butterfly is sometimes mistaken for an owl? → (For more information about this butterfly, turn to page 11.)

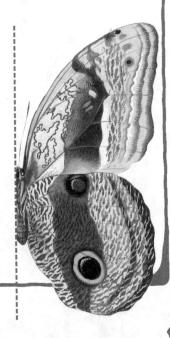

Next Step: You've probably learned about mirror images in science. Perhaps you've even talked about reflections, which are sometimes called flips, in your math class. Another way of making a mirror image is by folding a sheet of paper in half. Open the paper, and place drops of paint on one half of it (use two or three colors). Then, close the paper and press firmly. Immediately open the paper and see what looks like mirror images. In art, this is called *symmetry*.

Art Credits: top left: Elizabeth Morales-Denney; bottom right: Chuck Ripper, originally published in *Butterflies Zoobooks®*.

Answer: <u>A Royal Traveler</u>: The butterfly pictured is a monarch. You can learn more about it by reading pages 12 and 13.

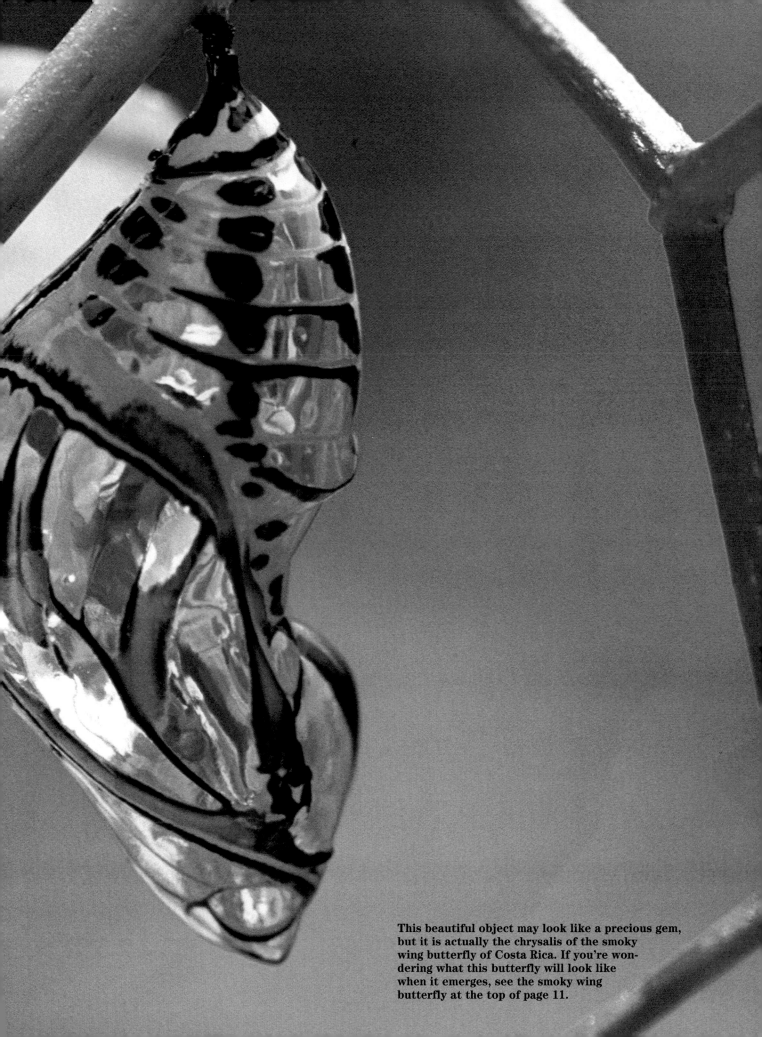

This beautiful object may look like a precious gem, but it is actually the chrysalis of the smoky wing butterfly of Costa Rica. If you're wondering what this butterfly will look like when it emerges, see the smoky wing butterfly at the top of page 11.

Butterflies and caterpillars are hunted by birds, lizards, monkeys, spiders, and many other animals. But they have some surprising ways to defend themselves and scare away predators. Most butterflies and caterpillars can blend in with their surroundings by looking like bark or leaves. Some resemble bad-tasting insects that predators don't like to eat. And a few are actually poisonous to predators. Predators know which species to avoid and take no chances with an expert mimic.

Other butterflies use their bright colors to startle attackers. Some have spots on their wings that look like giant eyes that might belong to a large animal. This can look scary to a predator. Still others release a bad odor that drives predators away. All in all, butterflies and caterpillars need many ways to escape danger, because predators lurk everywhere and can strike at any time!

The Indian leaf butterfly is a master of disguise. As you can see at left, it is very colorful with its wings open. But when it closes them, below, it looks just like a leaf on a tree.

Birds are the chief predators of butterflies. Because they can attack both in the air and on the ground, birds have more opportunities to catch butterflies than other animals do. So a butterfly that can look like a bigger, scarier bird might avoid being eaten.

The blue *Morpho*, above, flashes its shiny wings at would-be predators. The sudden, shimmering color startles the predator long enough for the butterfly to get away. Some other butterflies also use this *flash coloration*.

Some butterflies are mildly poisonous. When a predator eats one, it usually gets sick. After that, it remembers not to eat this kind of butterfly again. It will recognize the butterfly's distinct colors and patterns and avoid it. Poisonous butterflies are only harmful if they are eaten.

POISONOUS SMOKY WING BUTTERFLY

A butterfly has an advantage if it looks like a poisonous variety. Over time, some butterfly species have developed into look alikes. This is called *mimicry*. If you were a predator, would you think the moth and butterflies below were safe to eat?

NONPOISONOUS BUTTERFLIES

NONPOISONOUS MOTH

The hairstreak butterfly can't scare predators away, so it fools them! When threatened, it rubs its hind legs together and makes its trailing tails look like long antennae. Birds and other predators then nip the tails instead of the butterfly's head.

The eyespots on the wings of this owl butterfly from South America look like the eyes of an owl. And when it flaps its wings, the "eyes" look like they're blinking. This can scare away birds and other small animals that are afraid of owls.

Many caterpillars have eyespots on their skin that make them look like snakes. Some swallowtail caterpillars can even rear up at attackers to make themselves look more threatening!

Swallowtail caterpillars have the ultimate secret weapon — a Y-shaped fork in their heads called an *osmeterium*. This fork releases an unpleasant odor that sends predators scrambling. If the smell doesn't frighten them, the bright orange color usually does!

Some caterpillars have patterns that make them look like bird droppings — something no predator wants to eat.

11

Monarch butterflies travel, or *migrate*, thousands of miles each year. They begin to leave their Canadian breeding grounds in midsummer and by autumn they are in full force, flying south for the winter. In spring, they fly north again.

Many species of butterflies migrate to escape cold weather, but only the monarch butterfly of North America makes a *true* migration, flying south and north again in the same year, every year. Some populations travel as far as 4,000 miles round trip!

What makes this migration even more amazing is that few of the butterflies that begin the journey complete the round trip. Instead, it is a multi-generational relay race! Most of the returning butterflies are offspring that hatched and developed during the southern wintering period. The northbound flight is more grueling. The butterflies set off separately, flying day and night. They seldom rest or eat, but live off their stored fat. Later generations will find their way south the following year — visiting the same places and the same trees that their ancestors have visited year after year. The monarch migration is one of the mysteries of nature.

☐ OUTBOUND
☐ RETURN

ROCKY MOUNTAINS

Monarchs are well on their way to Florida, California, and Mexico before the autumn chill. Those *east* of the Rocky Mountains and bound for Mexico fly the farthest — more than 2,000 miles. Those *west* of the Rockies migrate about 1,000 miles to the California coast.

Eastern monarchs travel in swarms to the plains of Mexico. After several thousand have gathered, they fly high into the mountains. Every year, they stop to rest on the same fir trees.

Some scientists think that migrating monarchs have a built-in compass to point them in the right direction. Others believe that monarchs simply navigate by using the sun. How would you find your way home from a place you had never been before?

Monarchs can migrate to Mexico in two months or less, depending on the weather. Even though they have only a four-inch wingspan, monarchs can travel more than 1,000 miles in just a few days! They coast and glide to save energy, fill up on nectar along the way, and arrive far fatter than when they left!

How can an animal as tiny as a butterfly migrate so many thousands of miles? Scientists have discovered that one way monarchs do this is by hitching rides on winds, storms, and *even hurricanes* heading south! They glide on the wind currents, which carry them more than 7,000 feet above sea level. Airline pilots have reported seeing monarchs as high as 29,000 feet!

About *200 million* monarch butterflies spend their winter in a forest near Mexico City. Scientists estimate that there are as many as 10 million butterflies per acre in this forest! At times, the trees are literally covered with monarchs.

The farther south they go, the choosier monarchs become about the winds they ride. They prefer winds that are going toward their southern resting ground.

Scientists tag monarchs to study them. This is a delicate operation. First, a small area at the top of the wing is gently brushed with the fingertips to clear it of scales. Then a tiny piece of adhesive paper is attached to the wing.

It wasn't until the mid-1970s that scientists discovered where all the millions of eastern monarchs were gathering in Mexico. Scientists now capture, weigh, tag, and release both eastern and western monarchs to learn more about their remarkable migration.

EIGHTY-EIGHT BUTTERFLY
(South America)

Thousands of butterfly species have become extinct in the last 50 years, most of them in the tropics. On these pages, you can see some of the most stunning and colorful of the living tropical species—from the dazzling giant blue Hercules with its shimmering blue wings to the spectacular birdwings and swallowtails.

TROPICAL SKIPPER
(Africa)

AFRICAN GIANT SWALLOWTAIL
(Africa)

FORMOSISSIMA SKIPPER
(Africa)

GREAT BLUE HAIRSTREAK
(Ecuador)

BANANA EATER
(New Guinea)

CHIMAERA BIRDWING
(Papua New Guinea)

Butterflies are the jewels of the tropical rain forests. Ten thousand butterfly species populate the rain forests of South America and Central America alone. Flowering plants flourish in the rain forest's warm, damp climate, and butterflies flit from one to another, unfurling their coiled proboscises to drink sweet nectar. Butterfly eggs are placed on the appropriate leaves so the hatching caterpillar can gorge itself until it becomes encased in its chrysalis to emerge as a beautiful butterfly.

But the tropical rain forests are in danger, and that puts butterflies and other wildlife in danger, too. When people clear huge areas of forest to sell timber or to farm, the animals have no home. When farmers destroy the caterpillars that eat their plants, they disrupt the life cycle that would produce a butterfly. Sadly, the beautiful tropical species are the most endangered of all butterflies.

THOAS SWALLOWTAIL
(South and Central America)

Every minute, an area of rain forest as large as 40 to 50 football fields disappears. Half of all animal and plant species in the world live in the tropical forests—*many not yet discovered!* The species destroyed with the forests represent natural medicines and new food sources that we will never know. And many beautiful butterflies will be lost forever.

PRIAMUS BIRDWING
(New Guinea)

Some countries, like Taiwan, have made butterfly collecting into a major industry. Although the Taiwanese export 15 million specimens a year, there is no decline in the butterfly population. Why? Because most of the butterflies are collected after they have laid their eggs.

MALAY LACEWING
(Malaysia)

GIANT BLUE HERCULES
(Papua New Guinea)

HELICONIUS BUTTERFLY
(South America)

AGRIAS BUTTERFLY
(Brazil)

HOMERUS SWALLOWTAIL
(Jamaica)

Brazil, New Guinea, and other tropical countries sell hundreds of millions of butterflies to collectors each year. Fortunately, many of these specimens are raised on butterfly farms instead of being collected from the wild. More and more people are beginning to realize that butterfly farms, like the one above, can help save many species of butterflies.

With more than two million specimens, the British Museum of Natural History holds the largest butterfly collection in the world. But smaller butterfly collections, like the one at left, can be found in shops and museums all over the world. Collections such as these help scientists identify and better understand butterflies. And they also help other people learn to care about butterflies.

*T*he future of tropical butterflies and other tropical species is linked to the future of the rain forest. While butterfly farms in many parts of the world help to conserve butterflies, they don't do much to save rainforest habitat. But in Costa Rica, a program called *Proyecto de Mariposas*, or "Butterfly Project," *does* help the rain forest.

For many years, the villagers of Barra del Colorado, Costa Rica, lived by fishing. Now, there are few fish for them to catch. Commercial fishermen from a neighboring country overfished the area by using large nets called *gill nets* that trap great numbers of fish at one time. With no fish, the people of Barra del Colorado became very poor. Today, they are learning to use some resources of the rain forest in a way that won't deplete them. This is called *sustainable resource use*. It allows people to benefit from nature and encourages them to be its caretakers.

The rain forest of Barra del Colorado was logged 50 to 75 years ago. Its beautiful hardwood was made into furniture and wall paneling for people in other parts of the world. After a rain forest has been cut down, the soil erodes and loses its nutrients. It takes many years for the forest to grow back. Now there is strong regrowth in this rain forest. Villagers are being taught how to make a living from the forest without hurting it. They will farm butterflies to earn money and preserve the forest that is the source of the butterflies.

The *children* of Barra del Colorado convinced their parents that butterflies could improve their lives. A team from the Zoological Society of San Diego suggested *Proyecto de Mariposas* as a science project for the local school, which goes to the fourth grade. First, villagers cleared a garbage dump next to the school for the butterfly farm. Then they planted vegetation that would attract butterflies to lay their eggs and give caterpillars plenty to eat. The butterfly garden and nectar garden will benefit the community instead of enriching just a few.

Soon, the people of Barra del Colorado will be selling their butterflies to exporters in San Jose, the capital of Costa Rica. The children of Barra del Colorado have shown that with projects like these, people can live in harmony with nature.

AFRICAN MONARCH BUTTERFLIES